Also by Jaroslaw Jankowski

Why Are We So Different?
Your Guide to the 16 Personality Types

Why are we so very different from one another?
Why do we organise our lives in such disparate
ways? Why are our modes of assimilating
information so varied? Why are our approaches
to decision-making so diverse? Why are our
forms of relaxing and 'recharging our batteries'
so dissimilar?

Your Guide to the 16 Personality Types will help you
to understand both yourselves and other people
better. It will aid you not only in avoiding any
number of traps, but also in making the most of
your personal potential, as well as in taking the
right decisions about your education and career
and in building healthy relationships with others.
The book contains the ID16™© Personality
Test, which will enable you to determine your
own personality type. It also offers
a comprehensive description of each of the
sixteen types.

The Inspector

Your Guide
to the ISTJ Personality Type

The ID16$^{TM©}$ *Personality Types series*

JAROSLAW JANKOWSKI
M.Ed., EMBA

LOGOS MEDIA

This is a book which can help you exploit your potential more fully, build healthy relationships with other people and make the right decisions about your education and career. However, it should not be considered to be a substitute for expert physiological or psychiatric consultation. Neither the author nor the publisher accept any responsibility whatsoever for any detrimental effects which may result from the inappropriate use of this book.

ID16™© is an independent typology developed by Polish educator and manager Jaroslaw Jankowski and grounded in Carl Gustav Jung's theory. It should not be confused with the personality typologies and tests proposed by other authors or offered by other institutions.

Original title: Twój typ osobowości: Inspektor (ISTJ)
Translated from the Polish by Caryl Swift
Proof reading: Lacrosse | experts in translation
Layout editing by Zbigniew Szalbot

Published by LOGOS MEDIA

Paperback: ISBN 978-83-7981-075-8
EPUB: ISBN 978-83-7981-076-5
MOBI: ISBN 978-83-7981-077-2

Contents

Preface

The work in your hands is a compendium of knowledge on the *inspector*. It forms part of the *ID16*$^{TM©}$ *Personality Types* series, which consists of sixteen books on the individual personality types and *Who Are You? The ID16*$^{TM©}$ *Personality Test*, an introduction to the ID16$^{TM©}$ independent personality typology, which is based on the theory developed by Carl Gustav Jung.

As you explore this book on the *inspector*, you will find the answer to a number of crucial questions:

- How do *inspectors* think and what do they feel? How do they make decisions? How do they solve problems? What makes them anxious? What do they fear? What irritates them?

- Which personality types are they happy to encounter on their road through life and which ones do they avoid? What kind of friends, life partners and parents do they make? How do others perceive them?
- What are their vocational predispositions? What sort of work environment allows them to function most effectively? Which careers best suit their personality type?
- What are their strengths and what do they need to work on? How can they make the most of their potential and avoid pitfalls?
- Which famous people correspond to the *inspector*'s profile?

The book also contains the most essential information about the ID16$^{TM©}$ typology.

We sincerely hope that it will help you in coming to know yourself and others better.

ID16™© and Jungian Personality Typology

ID16™© numbers among what are referred to as Jungian personality typologies, which draw on the theories developed by Carl Gustav Jung (1875-19161), a Swiss psychiatrist and psychologist and a pioneer of the 'depth psychology' approach.

On the basis of many years of research and observation, Jung came to the conclusion that the differences in people's attitudes and preferences are far from random. He developed a concept which is highly familiar to us today: the division of people into extroverts and introverts. In addition, he distinguished four personality functions, which form two opposing pairs: sensing-intuition and thinking-feeling. He also established that one function is dominant in each pair. He became convinced that each and every person's dominant functions are fixed and independent of external conditions and that, together, what they form is a personality type.

In 1938, two American psychiatrists, Horace Gray and Joseph Wheelwright, created the first personality test based on Jung's theories. It was designed to make it possible to determine the dominant functions within the three dimensions described by Jung, namely, **extraversion-introversion**, **sensing-intuition** and **thinking-feeling**. That first test became the inspiration for other researchers. In 1942, again in America, Isabel Briggs Myers and Katherine Briggs began using their own personality test, broadening Gray's and Wheelwright's classic, three-dimensional model to include a fourth: **judging-perceiving**. The majority of subsequent personality typologies and tests drawing on Jung's theories also take that fourth dimension into account. They include the American typology published by David W. Keirsey in 1978 and the personality test developed in the nineteen seventies by Aušra Augustinavičiūtė, a Lithuanian psychologist. Over the following decades, other European researchers followed in their footsteps, creating more four-dimensional personality typologies and tests for use in personal coaching and career counselling.

ID16$^{TM©}$ figures among that group. An independent typology developed by Polish educator and manager Jaroslaw Jankowski, it was published in the first decade of the twenty-first century. ID16$^{TM©}$ is based on Carl Jung's classic theory and, like other contemporary Jungian typologies, it follows a four-dimensional path, terming those dimensions the **four natural inclinations**. These inclinations are dichotomous in nature and the picture they provide gives us information regarding a person's personality type. Analysis of the first inclination is intended to determine the dominant **source of life energy**, this being either the exterior or the interior world. Analysis of the second inclination defines the dominant **mode of assimilating information**, which occurs via the senses or via intuition. Analysis of the third inclination supplies a description of the **decision-making mode**, where either mind or heart is dominant, while analysis of the fourth inclination produces a definition of the dominant **lifestyle** as either organised or spontaneous. The combination of all these natural inclinations results in **sixteen possible personality types**.

One remarkable feature of the ID16™© typology is its practical dimension. It describes the individual personality types in action – at work, in daily life and in interpersonal relations. It neither concentrates on the internal dynamics of personality nor does it undertake any theoretical attempts at explaining or commenting on invisible, interior processes. The focus is turned more toward the ways in which a given personality type manifests itself externally and how it affects the surrounding world. This emphasis on the social aspect of personality places ID16™© somewhat closer to the previously mentioned typology developed by Aušra Augustinavičiūtė.

Each of the ID16™© personality types is the result of a given person's natural inclinations.

There is nothing evaluative or judgemental about ascribing a person to a given type, though. No particular personality type is 'better' or 'worse' than any other. Each type is quite simply different and each has its own potential strengths and weaknesses. ID16$^{TM©}$ makes it possible to identify and describe those differences. It helps us to understand ourselves and discover our place in the world.

Familiarity with our personality profile enables us to make full use of our potential and work on the areas which might cause us trouble. It is an invaluable aid in everyday life, in solving problems, in building healthy relationships with other people and in making decisions relating to our education and careers.

Determining personality is a process which is neither arbitrary nor mechanical in nature. As the 'owner and user' of our personality, each and every one of us is fully capable of defining which type we belong to. The individual's role is thus pivotal. This self-identification can be achieved either by analysing the descriptions of the ID16$^{TM©}$ personality types and steadily narrowing down the fields of choice or by taking the short cut provided by the ID16$^{TM©}$ Personality Test.[1] The role played by each 'personality user' is equally crucial when it comes to the test, given that the outcome depends entirely on the answers they provide.

---

[1] The test can be found in *Why Are We So Different? Your Guide to the 16 Personality Types* by Jaroslaw Jankowski.

Identifying personality types helps us to know both ourselves and others. Nonetheless, it should not be treated as some kind of future-determining oracle. No personality type can ever justify our weaknesses or poor interpersonal relationships. It might, however, help us to understand their causes!

ID16™© treats personality type not as a static, genetic, pre-determined condition, but as a product of innate and acquired characteristics. As such, it is a concept which neither diminishes free will nor engages in pigeonholing people. What it does is open up new perspectives for us, encouraging us to work on ourselves and indicating the areas where that work is most needed.

The Inspector (ISTJ)

The Personality in a Nutshell

Life motto: Duty first.

In brief, *inspectors* …

are people who can always be counted on. Well-mannered, punctual, reliable, conscientious and responsible, when they give their word, they keep it. Being analytical, methodical, systematic and logical by nature, they tend be seen as serious, cold and reserved. They prize calm, stability and order, have no fondness for change and like clear principles and concrete rules.

Inspectors are hard-working, persevering and capable of seeing things through to the end. As perfectionists, they try to exercise control over everything within their sphere and are sparing in their praise. They also underrate the importance of other people's feelings and emotions.

The *inspector's* four natural inclinations:

- source of life energy: the interior world
- mode of assimilating information: via the senses
- decision-making mode: the mind
- lifestyle: organised

Similar personality types:

- the Practitioner
- the Administrator
- the Animator

Statistical data:

- *inspectors* constitute between six and ten per cent of the global community
- men predominate among *inspectors* (60 per cent)
- Switzerland is an example of a nation corresponding to the *inspector's* profile[2]

---

[2] What this means is not that all the residents of Switzerland fall within this personality type, but that Swiss society as a whole possesses a great many of the character traits typical of the *inspector*.

The Four-Letter Code

In terms of Jungian personality typology, the universal four-letter code for the *inspector* is ISTJ.

General character traits

Inspectors are patient, persevering, conscientious, hard-working and, given their natural love of order, well organised. Their sense of duty is their constant companion. They like clearly defined tasks and concrete guidelines, perceiving the world and their surroundings as a highly particular system which depends for its stability and proper functioning on people's acceptance of, and adherence to, the principles and rules in force.

Organisational modes

Inspectors are happy when things are proceeding as they should and thus subject everything within their sphere to unceasing inspection … hence the name for this personality type. They are quick to spot gaps, errors and defects. Capable of seeing things through to the end, they derive great satisfaction from completing a task and only then will they feel able to give themselves over to their next commitment. They have an intense dislike of unregulated duties, uncompleted tasks and unpaid bills, all of which disrupt their peace of mind.

They like life to be orderly and stable and derive great joy from small, simple things. Excellent managers of their time, they more often than not adhere to a fixed and constant 'plan for the day'. Their approach to their work is organised and systematic; they make a note of tasks to be done and are scrupulous about checking that none have been overlooked. It is rare indeed for them to be unprepared or for something to take them by surprise. Armed with a plan of action, they feel secure and ready to confront a variety of duties, responsibilities and challenges. On the other hand, they dislike changes intensely, especially those which have a major impact on their lives.

When it comes to lifestyle, the simple and natural suits them down to the ground. Prizing stability and security, they will do their utmost to avoid risky undertakings. They would rather solve present problems than become involved in predicting those which might arise in the future; their preference will always be for the concrete, the perceptible and the tangible.

Communication

When engaged in a discussion, *inspectors* call upon hard facts, concrete data and logic. Combined with their self-assured attitude, this approach means that they have the ability to convince people that they are right – even when they are wrong! In principle, they operate on the assumption that they are, indeed, in the right and struggle with making room for the notion that they might, in fact, be at least partially mistaken. Nonetheless, they will not attempt to prove their rightness at any price; if they see that doing so might give rise to conflict, they are capable of backing down from the confrontation.

As others see them

Inspectors are perceived as responsible, sensible, courteous and honest people who can always be counted on. The fact that they will always keep their word, their dependability and their punctuality all arouse widespread respect. However, they also have a reputation as being rather unapproachable. Their natural reticence not only makes them difficult to get to know, but also creates a problem when it comes to guessing what they might be thinking and feeling. They are frequently seen as serious, cold and reserved; indeed, some people feel ill-at-ease in their presence, since they often unconsciously engender a sense of inferiority, or even of guilt, in others, triggering a defensive reaction as a result.

Their scepticism and mistrust of new concepts and ideas can also pose a problem. They expect others to provide proof that their proposals for change or new solutions really do have a point. Indeed, when talking to *inspectors*, some people will feel that what they are involved in is less of a conversation and more of an interrogation. Their perfectionism, meticulous focus on detail, urge to control everything within their sphere and conviction that they are always right are also sources of irritation to others.

Aesthetics

Inspectors have no desire either to be surrounded by luxury or to pursue the latest trends, focusing instead on the functional attributes of objects, preferring simple, practical things which are inexpensive to use and prizing their reliability and durability. Elaborate décor, ostentation and sophistication hold no attraction for them; their homes and work stations are usually cared for, functional and tastefully furnished. Tending more towards the traditional in their dress and steering well clear of experiment and flamboyance themselves, they find people who buy clothes or objects simply because they are 'on-trend' a source of utter bewilderment.

Perception and thinking

Inspectors rely on the input of their five senses and are never really guided by emotions, fleeting feelings or impulses. Their decision-making process is logical, rational and grounded in hard data and facts. They are able to express their views clearly and convincingly and will readily do so in writing. The exterior world will never be as important to them as their own, interior one and they generally have a sense of being self-sufficient, assuming that other people have little to offer them. By the same token, understanding opinions and behaviour which differ significantly from their own presents them with a serious problem.

Leisure

Although *inspectors* are devoted to their work, they are also capable of relaxing and are aided in that by their excellent organisational skills. They approach leisure with the same attitude that they bring to their other tasks; their free time is arranged in an orderly fashion and their holidays are thoroughly thought-out and planned, leaving little room for surprises, spontaneity or improvisation.

In the face of stress

Inspectors employ a mechanism inherent to their nature when they attempt to defend themselves against stress; they are, *de facto*, better at avoiding it than they are at coping with it. During particularly tense periods, they tend to sketch out black scenarios in their minds, envisaging their employer collapsing into bankruptcy, while they lose their jobs as a consequence, imagining the onset of disease, be it in themselves or those closest to them, blaming themselves for not having done something as it should have been done or succumbing to an overwhelming sense of their own incompetence and sinking into decision-making paralysis. Under the influence of long-term stress, the spiritual calm so typical of them may vanish, along with their ability to assess situations coolly and logically. They might also experience surges of nostalgia.

Socially

As *inspectors* see it, responsibility and loyalty are the crucial elements cementing interpersonal relations. They themselves express their affection and love through deeds and neither perceiving the emotions and needs of others nor voicing their own comes naturally to them. However, their powerful sense of duty often saves them here; once they become aware of other people's needs, they will view fulfilling them as their bounden duty and they are then capable of showing interest, concern and care.

Although they have an intense dislike of purely social gatherings, they do enjoy family celebrations; indeed, maintaining family traditions matters to them greatly. Amongst family and close friends, they display the ability to joke and amuse others with their conversation. They are exceptionally loyal to their employer, their family and their close friends and are often involved in the life of their neighbourhood or their village, town or city. For *inspectors*, the places that count for the most are their work, their homes and their local community.

Amongst friends

Inspectors feel perfectly at home among other people, though they dislike being the centre of attention. Sparing of words by nature, they find intensive conversations extremely draining and they have an absolute need for solitary moments which will allow them to relax and think current matters over in peace and quiet.

On the one hand, they are perceived as extremely serious; on the other hand, their friends are familiar with another side to their character, as people who know how to have fun and joke around. *Inspectors* see their friendships as highly important and they nurture them solicitously, investing enormous energy in them. However, although they willingly devote themselves to their friends, their family will always come first. They most often strike up friendships with *practitioners*, *administrators*, *strategists* and other *inspectors*. They find the carefree approach exhibited by *enthusiasts*, *idealists* and *counsellors* irritating in the extreme; an aversion which is, in fact, mutual, since those personality types perceive *inspectors* as being overly reserved, rigid and conservative.

As life partners

Care and concern for their nearest and dearest, their security and their material needs are viewed by *inspectors* as their patently obvious duty. In their eyes, the commitments and promises they make are sacred and they consider the vow "until death us do part" in exactly the same way. As a rule, their relationship with their life partner is precisely that: a relationship for life.

Inspectors are not overly burdened with emotional needs. They themselves expect little from their partner in the way of warm words, compliments or gestures of affection and are unlikely to identify those needs in others. Indeed, displaying warmth and affection is problematic for them; their mode of expressing love and attachment is through concrete action and they are numbered among those who tend to buy those closest to them practical gifts, for instance.

The natural candidates for an *inspector's* life partner are people of a personality type akin to their own: *practitioners*, *administrators* or *animators*. Building mutual understanding and harmonious relations will be easier in a union of that kind. Nonetheless, experience has taught us that people are also capable of creating happy and successful relationships despite what would seem to be an evident typological incompatibility. Moreover, the differences between two partners can lend added dynamics to a relationship and engender personal development. Indeed, for many people, this is a prospect that appears more attractive than the vision of a harmonious relationship in which concord and full, mutual understanding hold sway.

Inspectors' diligence and reliability arouses the respect both of their nearest and dearest and of those around them in general. Yet their professional success comes at a cost, since they will normally treat their job as one of their priorities in life and have great difficulty in completely compartmentalising their working and personal lives. Their directness represents another potential problem in their relationships with those closest to them and their critical remarks may well hurt their partner, while they themselves remain absolutely unaware of having done so. In general, they lack the ability both to put themselves in other people's shoes and to predict how a given mode of behaviour or choice of words can upset them.

Whatever their role in society, be it as a child, a life partner, a friend, a parent or a colleague, *inspectors* have a driving urge to perform it in the very best way possible. Given that their sense of responsibility is always their motivating force, their success in any area will invariably depend upon whether or not they consider the matter in question to be their duty. So, once they acknowledge that meeting the emotional needs of their nearest and dearest is their responsibility, they will throw themselves wholeheartedly into their efforts to fulfil it – and to their utmost abilities, at that.

As parents

Inspectors make highly conscientious and devoted parents, ready to invest every effort in bringing up their children in a positive and healthy atmosphere, ensuring that they want for nothing, and providing them with a stable, secure future, seeing this as their natural duty and endeavouring to discharge it to the full. They teach their offspring to perform their social roles and observe the prevailing norms and traditions, require their respect and tolerate neither disobedience nor the breaking of established rules. In general, they make high demands and are capable of severity, viewing discipline as a natural necessity and a tool assisting them to raise their children to be respectable, reliable and responsible adults.

Unstinting in their criticism, *inspectors* are also sparing when it comes to praising their offspring and, being unperceptive of their emotional needs, they tend to fail when it comes to demonstrating a sufficient amount of warmth. What this can generate is not only distance in terms of their parent-child relationships, but also a host of serious emotional problems in the children themselves. Fortunately, in numerous cases, once the *inspector* parent becomes aware of their offspring's needs, they begin to treat encouragement and positive reinforcement as a vital parental task, and that, in turn, serves as a natural spur to putting them into practice.

Their children will often view both the household norms and rules established by *inspectors,* as well as the consistency with which they enforce them, as oppressive, particularly during adolescence. However, those same norms and rules provide them with a sense of security and contribute to their social development. As adults, they appreciate their *inspector* parents for having assured them of a secure home, teaching them to behave responsibly, caring about their future and being ever at the ready in their devotion.

Work and career paths

Inspectors have the ability to perform tasks demanding adherence to complicated procedures, filling in forms and 'communing' with large quantities of numerical data. They will always put duty first and are incapable of relaxing or giving themselves over to pleasure when they have an important job hanging over their heads.

As part of a team

Inspectors like to operate independently and be evaluated on the basis of their own achievements. Nonetheless, if the situation demands it, they are capable of working in a group, though preferably with people who, like themselves, are properly organised and driven by the urge to fulfil their duties to the very best of their abilities.

They appreciate superiors who provide their staff with support and clear guidelines as regards accomplishing their tasks. As members of a team, they nurture a high standard of work and call attention to any details which have escaped the attention of their colleagues. People who fail to throw themselves wholeheartedly into their work and identify with their organisation's aims are a closed book to them. They are also unhappy in the midst of those who are emotional, irritable or given to wasting time on inessential discussions. Equally incomprehensible to them are people who knowingly break the rules, fail to keep their word, fail to return things they have borrowed, fail to fulfil their duties and responsibilities, or are only too happy to air their thoughts on matters which they are, in fact, clueless about.

Work style

Inspectors plan their work scrupulously and then consistently see things through to the end, doggedly making their way towards their goal and refusing to be disheartened by obstacles and difficulties which would discourage many another. Incapable of consciously working to less than their full potential, once a task is finished they will often give way to regret that they failed to do it better.

They prefer to work to step-by-step instructions which set out what needs doing and how it should be done, and they also hold tried and tested procedures and methods in high esteem. Indeed, when their intention is to convince others to employ a particular solution, they will often cite tradition and prior experience: "This is how it's always been done".

Inspectors dislike abstract theories and general concepts which lead to no clear, practical conclusions, and they are no more fond of tasks which are utterly different from what they have done previously and which cannot be solved on the basis of previous experience. They cope badly with radical changes, preferring those which either evolve or are made slowly and steadily. Although reluctant to accept innovation and experiment, they can be persuaded to come round to new methods or solutions if there is convincing proof of their benefits or if they have already been put to the test elsewhere.

Tasks

When *inspectors* are entrusted with a task, rest assured! It will be accomplished in line with the instructions and on time or, more often than not, ahead of time. As they see it, commitments, promises and deadlines are sacred. When they work on a task, they will usually spare neither time nor energy; indeed, even their health then takes a back seat. Their superiors, colleagues and business partners know they can be counted on. At the same time, although they might be overburdened already, *inspectors* will rarely refuse to take on more tasks, viewing their commitment as something absolutely normal. The pursuit of rewards and praise is as alien to them as broadcasting their own achievements. In fact, when they attain something remarkable, they are often completely unaware of having done so.

In positions of authority

Inspectors' commitment, diligence and reliability often pave the way for their promotion and they will frequently work their way up to supervisory and management positions. Once there, they establish clear rules and allocate precisely defined tasks to their staff, exhibit zero tolerance for wastefulness and inefficiency and find carelessness, unreliability and a dismissive or irreverent attitude towards tasks infuriating. When faced with unproductive and poor employees, they are capable of taking radical steps to improve the situation.

Companies and institutions

Inspectors fit in well in institutions with a long tradition, an established position and a fixed order. With their preference for employers who value their dedication, efforts and years of professional experience and who provide their staff with security and financial stability, they can often be found in public administration, large corporations and the uniformed services.

Professions

Knowledge of our own personality profile and natural preferences provides us with invaluable help in choosing the optimal path in our professional careers. Experience has shown that, while *inspectors* are perfectly able to work and find fulfilment in a range of fields, their personality type naturally predisposes them to the following fields and professions:

- administrator
- archivist
- the armed forces
- auditor
- aviator
- bookkeeper

- chartered accountant
- clerk
- computer programmer
- computer systems analyst
- financial controller
- detective
- engineer
- entrepreneur
- executive director
- farmer
- financial director
- inspector
- IT specialist
- judge
- lawyer
- librarian
- logistics
- manager
- mechanic
- pharmacist
- physician
- police officer
- science teacher
- technician

Potential strengths and weaknesses

Like any other personality type, *inspectors* have their potential strengths and weaknesses and this potential can be cultivated in a variety of ways. *Inspectors'* personal happiness and professional fulfilment depend on whether they make the most of the 'pluses' offered by their personality type and face up to its inherent dangers. Here, then, is a SUMMARY of those 'pluses' and dangers:

Potential strengths

Inspectors love order and hold tradition and rules in great respect. True to their word, loyal and steadfast, they take their responsibilities extremely seriously, care for their families and are ready to devote themselves to those closest to them. Their reliability, punctuality and ability to stick to a deadline all arouse the respect of others. Quick to spot gaps, errors and oversights, they are hard-working to a fault and always see things through to the end, without allowing obstacles to discourage them – an attitude which means that they usually attain their goals. They are capable of performing work which demands that they adhere to a host of procedures, process large quantities of data and carry out myriad routine activities.

Sharing their knowledge and experience with other people and helping them to resolve concrete problems is something they do willingly. Capable of expressing their thoughts and voicing their opinions clearly and matter-of-factly, they have little difficulty in convincing others that they are right. They cope well in situations of conflict and are open to constructive criticism from other people; it neither upsets them nor do they see it as a personal attack. At the same time, they are not easily dissuaded from their own views and opinions. When the need arises, they are able to discipline others and call their attention to shortcomings without feeling the need to tread delicately. They are excellent at managing money.

Potential weaknesses

Reading the feelings of others and perceiving their emotional needs is problematic for *inspectors*. Sparing in their praise, they also struggle when it comes to expressing love and affection. Their colleagues and those closest to them are often wearied by their driving urge to set everything in their sphere in order and then control it.

Assuming that they are always right, they tend to be premature in ruling out alternative solutions and other points of view. Looking at problems from a wider perspective and understanding opinions which differ from their own is also difficult for them and they will often dismiss other people's views in advance, without even trying to hear them out. When confronted by a problem, they have a tendency to blame others.

They cope badly with change and new situations. Their natural predilection for keeping strictly to guidelines, instructions and procedures can prove limiting in numerous circumstances, while their inclination to rely on previous experience and tried and tested solutions becomes an obstacle when they encounter new tasks requiring an approach which departs from the norm.

Personal development

Inspectors' personal development depends on the extent to which they make use of their natural potential and surmount the dangers inherent in their personality type. What follows are some practical indicators which, together, form a specific guide that we might call *The Inspector's Ten Commandments*.

Don't condemn others to relying on guesswork

Tell people how you feel and what you are going through. Give voice to your emotions. You will be helping your colleagues and your nearest and dearest immensely when you do. Whatever you say, it will usually be better than remaining silent.

Look at problems from a wider perspective

Try to look at problems from a wider perspective and different angles … and through other people's eyes. Turn to others for their opinions, give various points of view consideration and keep different aspects of a matter in mind.

Appreciate the worth of creative ideas

Operating solely on the basis of dry facts and hard data brings a whole range of restrictions in its wake. Many a problem can only be solved by creative ideas, an innovative method – and even by intuition!

Leave some things to take their natural course

There is no way you can have everything under your personal control and no way you can manage to be in command of it all, either. Leave less important matters to take their natural course. Set less crucial decisions to one side. Stop putting all that effort into reforming other people. You will save a great deal of energy and avoid an equal amount of frustration.

Criticise less, praise more

Be more restrained in your criticism and more generous in your evaluation and praise of others. Show them some warmth and make the most of every occasion to say something nice to them. Then wait and see. The difference will come as a pleasant surprise!

Be more open to people

Being open to others is not synonymous with discarding your own convictions and viewpoints. Stop assuming that they have nothing of interest to offer. Before you reject someone else's ideas or opinions, give them some serious consideration and try to understand them.

Treat others kindly

People hate being seen as just a part of a system or a cog in a machine. They long for their emotions, feelings and enthusiasms to be perceived. So try to put yourself in their shoes and understand what they are going through, what fascinates them, what worries them and what they fear...

Start believing in a world which is more than just black and white

Things may be more complex than they seem to you. Your problems may not only be caused by others; they might also be caused, to some extent at least … by you! You might not always be in the right. Bring that thought to the forefront of your mind before you start accusing others or pointing out their mistakes and reproaching them.

Accept change

When you discard ideas which might bring about change or undermine the current order in advance, you are throwing away the opportunity for development and depriving yourself of countless valuable experiences. Change always brings a certain amount of risk with it, but it will usually be less than you expected.

Stop 'interrogating' people

When you talk to others, try to hold a conversation with them rather than bombarding them with questions – an approach which leaves some people with the impression that they are being interrogated.

Well-known figures

- **George Washington** (1732-1799); an American general and politician, the first president of the United States, considered to be the father of the American nation.

- **John D. Rockefeller** (1839-1937); an American entrepreneur and philanthropist, reportedly the richest man in history.
- **George H. W. Bush** (1924-2018); the 41st president of the United States and father of the 43rd president, George W. Bush.
- **Queen Elizabeth II** (Elizabeth Alexandra Mary, of the House of Windsor; 1926-2022); the Head of State of the United Kingdom and fifteen other realms of the Commonwealth of Nations.
- **Warren Edward Buffett** (born in 1930); an American stock exchange investor, he is one of the richest men in the world.
- **Malcolm McDowell** (Malcolm John Taylor; born in 1943); a British screen actor whose filmography includes *A Clockwork Orange*.
- **Sting** (Gordon Matthew Sumner; born 1951); an English musician, singer-songwriter, activist, actor and philanthropist who first became known as the lead singer, bassist and principal songwriter for the new wave rock band The Police.
- **Condoleezza Rice** (born in 1954); an American politician, she holds a doctorate in political sciences. During President George W. Bush's presidency she served as the United States' 66th Secretary of State.
- **Gary Alan Sinise** (born in 1955); an American stage and screen actor whose

filmography includes the *CSI: NY* TV series, he is also a director, producer and musician.

- **Jackie Joyner-Kersee** (born in 1962); a record-breaking, world-class American athlete, now retired, she won numerous medals and is ranked as one of the best female athletes of all time.
- **Evander Holyfield** (born in 1962); a retired American boxer. Considered one of the greatest heavyweights ever, he earned himself the nickname of 'the Real Deal'.
- **Queen Rania of Jordan** (also known as Rania Al-Abdullah; born Raina al Yassin in 1970); consort to King Abdullah II of Jordan, she is a renowned social activist. In 2011, *Forbes* magazine ranked her as one of the hundred most powerful women in the world.

The ID16™© Personality Types in a Nutshell

The Administrator (ESTJ)

Life motto: We'll get the job done!

Administrators are hard-working, responsible and extremely loyal. Energetic and decisive, they value order, stability, security and clear rules. They are matter-of-fact and businesslike, logical, rational and practical and possess the capability to assimilate large amounts of detailed information.

Superb organisers, they are intolerant of ineffectuality, wastefulness and slothfulness. True to their convictions and direct in their contact with others, they present their point of view decisively and openly express critical opinions, sometimes hurting other people as a result.

The *administrator*'s four natural inclinations:

- source of life energy: the exterior world
- mode of assimilating information: via the senses
- decision-making mode: the mind
- lifestyle: organised

Similar personality types:

- the Animator
- the Inspector
- the Practitioner

Statistical data:

- *administrators* constitute between ten and thirteen per cent of the global community
- men predominate among *administrators* (60 per cent)
- the United States is an example of a nation corresponding to the *administrator's* profile[3]

Find out more!

The Administrator. Your Guide to the ESTJ Personality Type by Jaroslaw Jankowski

---

[3] What this means is not that all the residents of the USA fall within this personality type, but that American society as a whole possesses a great many of the character traits typical of the *administrator*.

The Advocate (ESFJ)

Life motto: How can I help you?

Advocates are well-organised, energetic and enthusiastic. Practical, responsible and conscientious, they are sincere and exceptionally gregarious.

Advocates are perceptive of human feelings, emotions and needs. They value harmony and find criticism and conflict difficult to bear. With their sensitivity to any and every manifestation of injustice, prejudice or detriment to another, they are genuinely interested in other people's problems and take real delight in helping them and tending to their needs, while often neglecting their own. They have a tendency to do everything for others and can be vulnerable to manipulation.

The *advocate*'s four natural inclinations:

- source of life energy: the exterior world
- mode of assimilating information: via the senses
- decision-making mode: the heart
- lifestyle: organised

Similar personality types:

- the Presenter
- the Protector
- the Artist

Statistical data:

- *advocates* constitute between ten and thirteen per cent of the global community
- women predominate among *advocates* (70 per cent)
- Canada is an example of a nation corresponding to the *advocate's* profile

Find out more!

The Advocate. Your Guide to the ESFJ Personality Type by Jaroslaw Jankowski

The Animator (ESTP)

Life motto: Let's DO something!

Animators are energetic, active and enterprising. Fond of the company of others, they have the ability to enjoy the moment and are spontaneous, flexible and open to change.

Animators are inspirers and instigators, spurring others to act. Being logical, rational and pragmatic realists, they are wearied by abstract concepts and solutions for the future. Their focus is on solving concrete problems in the here and now. They have difficulties with organising and planning and can be impulsive, acting first and thinking later.

The *animator's* four natural inclinations:

- source of life energy: the exterior world
- mode of assimilating information: via the senses

- decision-making mode: the mind
- lifestyle: spontaneous

Similar personality types:

- the Administrator
- the Practitioner
- the Inspector

Statistical data:

- *animators* constitute between six and ten per cent of the global community
- men predominate among *animators* (60 per cent)
- Australia is an example of a nation corresponding to the *animator's* profile

Find out more!

The Animator. Your Guide to the ESTP Personality Type by Jaroslaw Jankowski

The Artist (ISFP)

Life motto: Let's create something!

Artists are sensitive, creative and original, with a sense of the aesthetic and natural artistic talents. Independent in character, they follow their own system of values and are optimistic in outlook, with a positive approach to life and an ability to enjoy the moment.

Helping others is a source of joy to them. They find abstract theories tedious and would rather create reality than talk about it, although starting on something new comes more easily to them than finishing what they have already started. They have difficulty in voicing their own desires and needs.

The *artist's* four natural inclinations:

- source of life energy: the interior world
- mode of assimilating information: via the senses
- decision-making mode: the heart
- lifestyle: spontaneous

Similar personality types:

- the Protector
- the Presenter
- the Advocate

Statistical data:

- *artists* constitute between six and nine per cent of the global community
- women predominate among *artists* (60 per cent)
- China is an example of a nation corresponding to the *artist's* profile

Find out more!

The Artist. Your Guide to the ISFP Personality Type by Jaroslaw Jankowski

The Counsellor (ENFJ)

Life motto: My friends are my world

Counsellors are optimistic, enthusiastic and quick-witted. Courteous and tactful, they have an extraordinary gift for empathy and find joy in acting for the good of others, with no thought of themselves. They have the ability to influence other people, inspiring them, eliciting their hidden potential and giving them faith in their own powers. Radiating warmth, they draw others to them and often help them in solving their personal problems.

Counsellors can be over-trusting and have a tendency to view the world through rose-tinted glasses. With their focus on other people, they often forget about their own needs.

The *counsellor's* four natural inclinations:

- source of life energy: the exterior world
- mode of assimilating information: intuition
- decision-making mode: the heart
- lifestyle: organised

Similar personality types:

- the Enthusiast
- the Mentor
- the Idealist

Statistical data:

- *counsellors* constitute between three and five per cent of the global community
- women predominate among *counsellors* (80 per cent)
- France is an example of a nation corresponding to the *counsellor's* profile

Find out more!

The Counsellor. Your Guide to the ENFJ Personality Type by Jaroslaw Jankowski

The Director (ENTJ)

Life motto: I'll tell you what you need to do.

Directors are independent, active and decisive. Rational, logical and creative, when they analyse problems they look at the wider picture and are able to foresee the future consequences of human activities. They are characterised by optimism and a healthy sense of their own worth and are capable of transforming theoretical concepts into concrete, practical plans of action.

Visionaries, mentors and organisers, *directors* possess natural leadership skills. Their powerful personalities and direct and critical style can often have an intimidating effect, causing them problems in their interpersonal relationships.

The *director's* four natural inclinations:

- source of life energy: the exterior world

- mode of assimilating information: intuition
- decision-making mode: the mind
- lifestyle: organised

Similar personality types:

- the Innovator
- the Strategist
- the Logician

Statistical data:

- *directors* constitute between two and five per cent of the global community
- men predominate among *directors* (70 per cent)
- Holland is an example of a nation corresponding to the *director's* profile

Find out more!

The Director. Your Guide to the ENTJ Personality Type by Jaroslaw Jankowski

The Enthusiast (ENFP)

Life motto: We'll manage!

Enthusiasts are energetic, enthusiastic and optimistic. Capable of enjoying life and looking ahead to the future, they are dynamic, quick-witted and creative. They have a liking for people in general, value honest and genuine relationships and are warm, sincere and emotional. Criticism is something they handle badly. With their gift for empathy and ability to perceive people's needs, feelings and motives, they both inspire others and infect them with their own enthusiasm.

They love to be at the centre of events and are flexible and capable of improvising. Their inclination leads towards idealistic notions. Being easily distracted, they have problems with seeing things through to the end.

The *enthusiast's* four natural inclinations:

- source of life energy: the exterior world
- mode of assimilating information: intuition
- decision-making mode: the heart
- lifestyle: spontaneous

Similar personality types:

- the Counsellor
- the Idealist
- the Mentor

Statistical data:

- *enthusiasts* constitute between five and eight per cent of the global community
- women predominate among *enthusiasts* (60 per cent)
- Italy is an example of a nation corresponding to the *enthusiast's* profile

Find out more!

The Enthusiast. Your Guide to the ENFP Personality Type by Jaroslaw Jankowski

The Idealist (INFP)

Life motto: We CAN live differently.

Idealists are sensitive, loyal, and creative. Living in accordance with the values they hold is of immense importance to them and they both manifest an interest in the reality of the spirit and delve deeply into the mysteries of life. Wrapped up in the world's problems and open to the needs of other people, they prize harmony and balance.

Idealists are romantic; not only are they able to show love, but they also need warmth and affection themselves. With their outstanding ability to read other people's feelings and emotions, they build healthy, profound and enduring relationships. They feel that they are on very shaky ground in situations of conflict and have no real resistance to stress and criticism.

The *idealist's* four natural inclinations:

- source of life energy: the interior world
- mode of assimilating information: intuition
- decision-making mode: the heart
- lifestyle: spontaneous

Similar personality types:

- the Mentor
- the Enthusiast
- the Counsellor

Statistical data:

- *idealists* constitute between one and four per cent of the global community
- women predominate among *idealists* (60 per cent)
- Thailand is an example of a nation corresponding to the *idealist's* profile

Find out more!

The Idealist. Your Guide to the INFP Personality Type by Jaroslaw Jankowski

The Innovator (ENTP)

Life motto: How about trying a different approach…?

Innovators are inventive, original and independent. Optimistic, energetic and enterprising, they are people of action who love being at the centre of events and solving 'insoluble' problems. Their thoughts are turned to the future and they are curious about the world and visionary by nature. Open to new concepts and ideas, they enjoy new experiences and experiments and have the ability to identify the connections between separate events.

Innovators are spontaneous, communicative and self-assured. However, they tend to overestimate their own possibilities and have problems with seeing things through to the end. They are also inclined to be impatient and to take risks.

The *innovator's* four natural inclinations:

- source of life energy: the exterior world
- mode of assimilating information: intuition
- decision-making mode: the mind
- lifestyle: spontaneous

Similar personality types:

- the Director
- the Logician
- the Strategist

Statistical data:

- *innovators* constitute between three and five per cent of the global community
- men predominate among *innovators* (70 per cent)
- Israel is an example of a nation corresponding to the *innovator's* profile

Find out more!

The Innovator. Your Guide to the ENTP Personality Type by Jaroslaw Jankowski

The Inspector (ISTJ)

Life motto: *Duty first.*

Inspectors are people who can always be counted on. Well-mannered, punctual, reliable, conscientious and responsible, when they give their word, they keep it. Being analytical, methodical, systematic and logical by nature, they tend be seen as serious, cold and reserved. They prize calm, stability and order, have no fondness for change and like clear principles and concrete rules.

Inspectors are hard-working, persevering and capable of seeing things through to the end. As perfectionists, they try to exercise control over everything within their sphere and are sparing in their praise. They also underrate the importance of other people's feelings and emotions.

The *inspector's* four natural inclinations:

- source of life energy: the interior world
- mode of assimilating information: via the senses
- decision-making mode: the mind
- lifestyle: organised

Similar personality types:

- the Practitioner
- the Administrator
- the Animator

Statistical data:

- *inspectors* constitute between six and ten per cent of the global community
- men predominate among *inspectors* (60 per cent)
- Switzerland is an example of a nation corresponding to the *inspector's* profile

Find out more!

The Inspector. Your Guide to the ISTJ Personality Type by Jaroslaw Jankowski

The Logician (INTP)

Life motto: Above all else, seek to discover the truths about the world.

Logicians are original, resourceful and creative. With a love for solving problems of a theoretical nature, they are analytical, quick-witted, enthusiastically disposed towards new concepts and have the ability to connect individual phenomena, educing general rules and theories from them. Logical, exact and inquiring, they are quick to spot incoherence and inconsistency.

Logicians are independent, sceptical of existing solutions and authorities, tolerant and open to new challenges. When immersed in thought, they will sometimes lose touch with the outside world.

The *logician's* four natural inclinations:

- source of life energy: the interior world

- mode of assimilating information: intuition
- decision-making mode: the mind
- lifestyle: spontaneous

Similar personality types:

- the Strategist
- the Innovator
- the Director

Statistical data:

- *logicians* constitute between two and three per cent of the global community;
- men predominate among *logicians* (80 per cent)
- India is an example of a nation corresponding to the *logician's* profile

Find out more!

The Logician. Your Guide to the INTP Personality Type by Jaroslaw Jankowski

The Mentor (INFJ)

Life motto: The world CAN be a better place!

Mentors are creative and sensitive. With their gaze fixed firmly on the future, they spot opportunities and potential imperceptible to others. Idealists and visionaries, they are geared towards helping people and are conscientious, responsible and, at one and the same time, courteous, caring and friendly. They strive to understand the mechanisms governing the world and view problems from a wide perspective.

Superb listeners and observers, *mentors* are characterised by their extraordinary empathy, intuition and trust of people and are capable of reading the feelings and emotions of others. They find criticism and conflict difficult to bear and can come across as enigmatic.

The *mentor's* four natural inclinations:

- source of life energy: the interior world
- mode of assimilating information: intuition
- decision-making mode: the heart
- lifestyle: organised

Similar personality types:

- the Idealist
- the Counsellor
- the Enthusiast

Statistical data:

- *mentors* constitute one per cent of the global community and are the most rarely occurring of the sixteen personality types
- women predominate among *mentors* (80 per cent)
- Norway is an example of a nation corresponding to the *mentor's* profile

Find out more!

The Mentor. Your Guide to the INFJ Personality Type by Jaroslaw Jankowski

The Practitioner (ISTP)

Life motto: Actions speak louder than words.

Practitioners are optimistic and spontaneous, with a positive approach to life. Reserved and independent, they hold true to their personal convictions and view external principles and norms with scepticism. They find abstract concepts and solutions for the future tiresome and would far rather roll up their sleeves and get to work on solving tangible and concrete problems.

Adapting well to new places and situations, they enjoy fresh challenges and risks and are capable of keeping a cool head in the face of threats and danger. Their general reticence and extreme reserve when it comes to expressing their opinions mean that other people may often find them impenetrable.

The *practitioner's* four natural inclinations:

- source of life energy: the interior world
- mode of assimilating information: via the senses
- decision-making mode: the mind
- lifestyle: spontaneous

Similar personality types:

- the Inspector
- the Animator
- the Administrator

Statistical data:

- *practitioners* constitute between six and nine per cent of the global community
- men predominate among *practitioners* (60 per cent)
- Singapore is an example of a nation corresponding to the *practitioner's* profile

Find out more!

The Practitioner. Your Guide to the ISTP Personality Type by Jaroslaw Jankowski

The Presenter (ESFP)

Life motto: Now is the perfect moment!

Presenters are optimistic, energetic and outgoing, with the ability to enjoy life and have fun to the full. Practical, flexible and spontaneous at one and the same time, they enjoy change and new experiences, coping badly with solitude, stagnation and routine.

With their liking for being at the centre of attention, they are natural-born actors and their speaking abilities arouse the interest and enthusiasm of their listeners. Focused as they are on the present moment, they will sometimes lose sight of their long-term aims and can also have problems with foreseeing the consequences of their actions.

The *presenter's* four natural inclinations:

- source of life energy: the exterior world
- mode of assimilating information: via the senses
- decision-making mode: the heart
- lifestyle: spontaneous

Similar personality types:

- the Advocate
- the Artist
- the Protector

Statistical data:

- *presenters* constitute between eight and thirteen per cent of the global community
- women predominate among *presenters* (60 per cent)
- Brazil is an example of a nation corresponding to the *presenter's* profile

Find out more!

The Presenter. Your Guide to the ESFP Personality Type by Jaroslaw Jankowski

The Protector (ISFJ)

Life motto: Your happiness matters to me.

Protectors are sincere, warm-hearted, unassuming, trustworthy and extraordinarily loyal. With their ability to perceive people's needs and their desire to help them, they will always put others first. Practical, well-organised and gifted with both an eye and a memory for detail, they are responsible, hard-working, patient, persevering and capable of seeing things through to the end.

Protectors set great store by tranquillity, stability and friendly relations with others and are skilled at building bridges between people. By the same token, they find conflict and criticism difficult to bear. Given their powerful sense of duty and their constant readiness to come to the aid of others, they can end up being used by people.

The *protector's* four natural inclinations:

- source of life energy: the interior world
- mode of assimilating information: via the senses
- decision-making mode: the heart
- lifestyle: organised

Similar personality types:

- the Artist
- the Advocate
- the Presenter

Statistical data:

- *protectors* constitute between eight and twelve per cent of the global population
- women predominate among *protectors* (70 per cent)
- Sweden is an example of a nation corresponding to the *protector's* profile

Find out more!

The Protector. Your Guide to the ISFJ Personality Type by Jaroslaw Jankowski

The Strategist (INTJ)

Life motto: I can certainly improve this.

Strategists are independent and outstandingly individualistic, with an immense seam of inner energy. Creative, inventive and resourceful, others perceive them as competent, self-assured and, at one and the same time, distant and enigmatic. No matter what they turn their attention to, they will always look at the bigger picture and they have a driving urge to improve the world around them and set it in order.

Well-organised, responsible, critical and demanding, they are difficult to knock off balance – and just as hard to please to the full. Reading the emotions and feelings of others is something they find very problematic.

The *strategist's* four natural inclinations:

- source of life energy: the interior world
- mode of assimilating information: intuition
- decision-making mode: the mind
- lifestyle: organised

Similar personality types:

- the Logician
- the Director
- the Innovator

Statistical data:

- *strategists* constitute between one and two per cent of the global community
- men predominate among *strategists* (80 per cent)
- Finland is an example of a nation corresponding to the *strategist's* profile

Find out more!

The Strategist. Your Guide to the INTJ Personality Type by Jaroslaw Jankowski

Additional information

The four natural inclinations

1. THE DOMINANT SOURCE OF LIFE
   ENERGY

   a. THE EXTERIOR WORLD
      People who draw their energy
      from outside. They need activity
      and contact with others and find
      being alone for any length of time
      hard to bear.

   b. THE INTERIOR WORLD
      People who draw their energy
      from their inner world. They need
      quiet and solitude and feel drained

when they spend any length of
time in a group.

2. THE DOMINANT MODE OF
    ASSIMILATING INFORMATION

    a. VIA THE SENSES
        People who rely on the five senses
        and are persuaded by facts and
        evidence. They have a liking for
        methods and practices which are
        tried and tested and prefer
        concrete tasks and are realists who
        trust in experience.

    b. VIA INTUITION
        People who rely on the sixth
        sense and are driven by what they
        'feel in their bones'. They have a
        liking for innovative solutions and
        problems of a theoretical nature
        and are characterised by a creative
        approach to their tasks and the
        ability to predict.

3. THE DOMINANT DECISION-
    MAKING MODE

    a. THE MIND
        People who are guided by logic
        and objective principles. They are
        critical and direct in expressing
        their opinions.

b. THE HEART
People who are guided by their feelings and values. They long for harmony and mutual understanding with others.

4. THE DOMINANT LIFESTYLE

a. ORGANISED
People who are conscientious and organised. They value order and like to operate according to plan.

b. SPONTANEOUS
People who are spontaneous and value freedom of action. They live for the moment and have no trouble finding their feet in new situations.

The approximate percentage of each personality type in the world population

Personality Type:	Proportion:
• The Administrator (ESTJ):	10-13%
• The Advocate (ESFJ):	10-13%
• The Animator (ESTP):	6-10%
• The Artist (ISFP):	6-9%
• The Counsellor (ENFJ):	3-5 %
• The Director (ENTJ):	2-5%

- The Enthusiast (ENFP): 5-8%
- The Idealist (INFP): 1-4%
- The Innovator (ENTP): 3-5%
- The Inspector (ISTJ): 6-10%
- The Logician (INTP): 2-3%
- The Mentor (INFJ): ca. 1%
- The Practitioner (ISTP): 6-9%
- The Presenter (ESFP): 8-13%
- The Protector (ISFJ): 8-12%
- The Strategist (INTJ): 1-2%

The approximate percentage of women and men of each personality type in the world population

Personality Type:	**Women / Men:**
The Administrator (ESTJ):	40% / 60%
The Advocate (ESFJ):	70% / 30%
The Animator (ESTP):	40% / 60%
The Artist (ISFP):	60% / 40%
The Counsellor (ENFJ):	80% / 20%
The Director (ENTJ):	30% / 70%
The Enthusiast (ENFP):	60% / 40%
The Idealist (INFP):	60% / 40%
The Innovator (ENTP):	30% / 70%
The Inspector (ISTJ):	40% / 60%
The Logician (INTP):	20% / 80%
The Mentor (INFJ):	80% / 20%
The Practitioner (ISTP):	40% / 60%
The Presenter (ESFP):	60% / 40%

- The Protector (ISFJ):   70% / 30%
- The Strategist (INTJ):   20% / 80%

Bibliography

- Arraj, Tyra & Arraj, James: *Tracking the Elusive Human, Volume 1: A Practical Guide to C.G. Jung's Psychological Types, W.H. Sheldon's Body and Temperament Types and Their Integration*, Inner Growth Books, 1988
- Arraj, James: *Tracking the Elusive Human, Volume 2: An Advanced Guide to the Typological Worlds of C. G. Jung, W.H. Sheldon, Their Integration, and the Biochemical Typology of the Future*, Inner Growth Books, 1990
- Berens, Linda V.; Cooper, Sue A.; Ernst, Linda K.; Martin, Charles R.; Myers, Steve; Nardi, Dario; Pearman, Roger R.; Segal, Marci; Smith, Melissa: *A Quick Guide to the 16 Personality Types in Organizations: Understanding Personality Differences in the Workplace*, Telos Publications, 2002

- Geier, John G. & Downey, E. Dorothy: *Energetics of Personality*, Aristos Publishing House, 1989

- Hunsaker, Phillip L. & Alessandra, Anthony J.: *The Art of Managing People*, Simon and Schuster, 1986

- Jung, Carl Gustav: *Psychological Types (The Collected Works of C. G. Jung, Vol. 6)*, Princeton University Press, 1976

- Kise, Jane A. G.; Stark, David & Krebs Hirsch, Sandra: *LifeKeys: Discover Who You Are*, Bethany House, 2005

- Kroeger, Otto & Thuesen, Janet: *Type Talk or How to Determine Your Personality Type and Change Your Life*, Delacorte Press, 1988

- Lawrence, Gordon: *People Types and Tiger Stripes*, Center for Applications of Psychological Type, 1993

- Lawrence, Gordon: *Looking at Type and Learning Styles*, Center for Applications of Psychological Type, 1997

- Maddi, Salvatore R.: *Personality Theories: A Comparative Analysis*, Waveland, 2001

- Martin, Charles R.: *Looking at Type: The Fundamentals Using Psychological Type To Understand and Appreciate Ourselves and Others*, Center for Applications of Psychological Type, 2001

- Meier C.A.: Personality: *The Individuation Process in the Light of C. G. Jung's Typology*, Daimon Verlag, 2007

- Pearman, Roger R. & Albritton, Sarah: *I'm Not Crazy, I'm Just Not You: The Real Meaning of the Sixteen Personality Types*, Davies-Black Publishing, 1997
- Segal, Marci: Creativity and Personality Type: *Tools for Understanding and Inspiring the Many Voices of Creativity*, Telos Publications, 2001
- Sharp, Daryl: Personality Type: *Jung's Model of Typology*, Inner City Books, 1987
- Spoto, Angelo: *Jung's Typology in Perspective*, Chiron Publications, 1995
- Tannen, Deborah: *You Just Don't Understand*, William Morrow and Company, 1990
- Thomas, Jay C. & Segal, Daniel L.: *Comprehensive Handbook of Personality and Psychopathology, Personality and Everyday Functioning*, Wiley, 2005
- Thomson, Lenore: *Personality Type: An Owner's Manual*, Shambhala, 1998
- Tieger, Paul D. & Barron-Tieger Barbara: *Just Your Type: Create the Relationship You've Always Wanted Using the Secrets of Personality Type*, Little, Brown and Company, 2000
- Von Franz, Marie-Louise & Hillman, James: *Lectures on Jung's Typology*, Continuum International Publishing Group, 1971

Putting the Reader first.

An Author Campaign Facilitated by ALLi.

www.ingramcontent.com/pod-product-compliance
Lightning Source LLC
Chambersburg PA
CBHW031209020426
42333CB00013B/852